ESSENTIAL
Energy

Energy from Fossil Fuels

Robert Snedden

www.heinemann.co.uk/library
Visit our website to find out more information about Heinemann Library books.

To order:
☎ Phone 44 (0) 1865 888066
▤ Send a fax to 44 (0) 1865 314091
▢ Visit the Heinemann Library Bookshop at www.heinemann.co.uk/library to browse our catalogue and order online.

First published in Great Britain by Heinemann Library,
Halley Court, Jordan Hill, Oxford OX2 8EJ
a division of Reed Educational and Professional Publishing Ltd.
Heinemann is a registered trademark of Reed Educational & Professional Publishing Ltd.

OXFORD MELBOURNE AUCKLAND
JOHANNESBURG BLANTYRE GABORONE
IBADAN PORTSMOUTH (NH) USA CHICAGO

Designed by Celia Floyd
Illustrated by Jeff Edwards and Alan Fraser
Originated by Ambassador Litho Ltd.
Printed in Hong Kong by Wing King Tong

ISBN 0 431 11760 8 (hardback)
06 05 04 03 02 01
10 9 8 7 6 5 4 3 2 1

ISBN 0 431 11765 9 (paperback)
07 06 05 04 03 02
10 9 8 7 6 5 4 3 2 1

British Library Cataloguing in Publication Data

Snedden, Robert
  Energy from fossil fuels. – (Essential energy)
  1. Fossil fuels
  I. Title
  333.8'2

Acknowledgements

The Publishers would like to thank the following for permission to reproduce photographs:
Austin J Brown/Aviation Picture Library: Pg.35; Camera Press: Pg.28, Pg.42; Corbis: Pg.4, Pg.9, Pg.18, Pg.19; Environmental Images: Pg.37, Pg.38, Pg.39; Hulton Deutsch: Pg.5; Hulton Getty: Pg.16, Pg.17; Mary Evans Picture Library: Pg.14, Pg.20, Pg.22; Paul Popper Ltd.: Pg.43; Robert Harding Picture Library: Pg.8, Pg.33; Science Photo Library: Pg.6, Pg.7, Pg.11, Pg.15, Pg.21, Pg.23, Pg.25, Pg.26, Pg.27, Pg.29, Pg.30, Pg.36, Pg.40, Pg.41; South American Pictures: Pg.13.

Cover photograph reproduced with permission of Photodisc.

Every effort has been made to contact copyright holders of any material reproduced in this book. Any omissions will be rectified in subsequent printings if notice is given to the Publisher.

Any words appearing in the text in bold, **like this**, are explained in the glossary.

Contents

Ancient sunlight

Energy makes things happen. It is the driving force of the Universe. Without energy there would be no Universe at all. In science, energy is the name given to the ability to do work. For a scientist, any activity involves work because all activities involve energy. Even when you are asleep your body is still at work, breaking down the food you eat, carrying out repairs and making new **cells**. A rock sitting motionless on the ground contains **chemical energy** that holds the **atoms** it is made of together, and atomic energy that holds together the particles that make up those atoms.

Life and energy

All life needs a source of energy. Most of the energy used by life on Earth comes from the Sun. In the remarkable process of **photosynthesis** green plants and some **micro-organisms** capture the Sun's energy and use it to make the food they need. The food that plants make for themselves in turn becomes the source of energy for all of the Earth's other organisms, which either eat plants or eat other animals that have eaten plants.

Without the Sun, the Earth would be a dark and lifeless rock.

People and energy

Much of the history of the human race has been about finding and controlling sources of energy. To begin with, people only had the strength of their own muscles to rely on. Later, the invention of agriculture and the domestication of animals provided another source of energy to draw on as animals could be used to plough fields and transport goods. Mastering the use of fire opened the way for people to make pottery, forge metals and cook food. Harnessing the energy of the wind to power sailing ships allowed people to travel along rivers and across seas.

This steam-powered locomotive makes use of the energy of the Sun stored in the coal it burns.

With the discovery of **fossil fuels** people found a new way of using the energy of the Sun. Coal, **petroleum** and **natural gas** all contain energy from the Sun that was trapped by living plants and micro-organisms many millions of years ago. Fossil fuels, in particular coal, powered the **Industrial Revolution** which eventually led to the high-technology society we live in today.

We still rely to an enormous extent on the ancient energy trapped in fossil fuels. We release the energy of petroleum in our aircraft and road vehicles. Many of us use natural gas to cook our food. Coal, oil and gas are all used to provide the energy needed to generate electricity in power stations.

This book tells the story of fossil fuels: how they were formed, how we obtain them, the wide variety of uses to which they are put and the consequences of using them.

Energy supply

We use energy in different forms to provide light and heat, to operate machinery, to prepare our food, to transport us from place to place and to make the things we need. All the usable energy we have available to carry out this work makes up our energy supply.

Sometimes we can obtain energy directly. For example, when you pluck an apple from a tree and eat it, you are making use of energy from the Sun, which the tree trapped and stored in the apple, to supply a part of your body's energy requirements. Often we will use energy indirectly, such as when we burn coal in a power station to heat water and turn it into steam; the steam is then used to spin a **turbine** that generates electricity, which we can put to a multitude of uses.

A section of the Trans-Alaskan oil pipeline that runs over 1200 kilometres across Alaska.

Essential fossil fuels

The world's chief sources of energy are, in order of importance, **fossil fuels**, water power and nuclear energy. Solar, wind, tidal and **geothermal** energy also provide some of our energy needs. More than 85 per cent of the energy produced by businesses and governments comes from fossil fuels (**petroleum**, coal and **natural gas**). These sources are called **fossil fuels** because they formed over millions of years from the fossilized remains of prehistoric plants.

The supply of fossil fuels is limited. Fossil fuels are a finite and nonrenewable resource. This means that once used, they cannot be recycled or replaced and eventually they will run out. Scientists and engineers are working to find ways of extracting the maximum yield from our fossil fuel resources and to develop other sources of energy to replace them.

Petroleum: Petroleum alone supplies 40 per cent of the world's major usage of energy, mostly to provide energy for transport and heating. Most petroleum is obtained from deep underground, on land or beneath the seafloor, as a liquid called **crude oil**. Refineries process the crude oil, breaking it down into kerosene, petrol (or gasoline) and other useful products.

Coal: Over a quarter (26 per cent), of the world's energy production comes from coal. Coal is used in the manufacture of steel, to produce the energy for steam engines and to generate electricity. In many parts of the world coal is used to provide heat for people's homes.

Natural gas: Natural gas supplies 21 per cent of the world's energy needs. It is used to generate electricity, for heating and cooking and sometimes for lighting.

Problems to solve

While fossil fuels have been essential in shaping our high-technology society, they continue to cause many problems. Spills from oil tankers pollute coastlines. Accidents and illnesses from breathing coal dust make coal mining a hazardous occupation. When burned, fossil fuels release carbon dioxide, a **greenhouse gas**, which many people believe is causing the Earth to warm up. Burning coal releases sulphur **compounds** and other impurities that cause **acid rain** and pollute the air. These problems cannot be ignored and a great deal of effort is being put into the search for answers.

Coal provides the energy for the fierce heat needed to make steel in a blast furnace.

Photosynthesis

Fossil fuels begin with sunlight. The process we have to thank for the fuels that power our cars and aircraft, heat our homes and cook our food is **photosynthesis**.

Photosynthesis is the biological process by which green plants, algae and some bacteria capture the energy of sunlight and use it to power the formation of glucose, a simple sugar, from carbon dioxide and water. Photosynthesis ultimately supplies nearly all of the energy used by life on Earth.

Chloroplasts

The entire process of photosynthesis occurs in chloroplasts, tiny green structures found mainly inside the leaf **cells** of green plants. Chloroplasts are generally 4 to 6 micrometres in length (a micrometre is a millionth of a metre) and are elliptical or disc-shaped. Each chloroplast contains chlorophyll, the pigment that gives the plant its green colour, and other chemicals necessary for photosynthesis. Photosynthesis depends on the ability of chlorophyll to capture the energy of sunlight and use it to split water **molecules**.

Microscopic structures inside a plant cell allow it to capture the energy of the Sun.

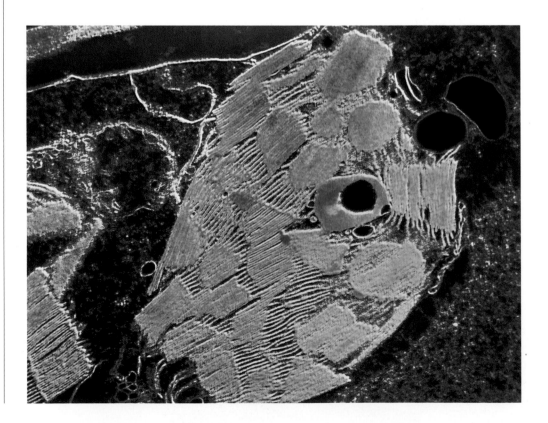

The chemical reactions involved in photosynthesis occur in two stages. During the light reaction, sunlight is used to split water into oxygen, hydrogen ions and electrons. In the dark reaction, for which sunlight is not required, the hydrogen ions and electrons are used to convert carbon dioxide into carbohydrates. The process can be summarized by a mathematical formula:

$$6CO_2 + 12H_2O + \text{sunlight} = C_6H_{12}O_6 + 6H_2O + 6O_2$$
(carbon dioxide + water + sunlight = glucose + water + oxygen)

Most of the glucose that forms during photosynthesis is stored in the chloroplasts as starch. As plant-eating animals eat the plant's leaves, they obtain their basic energy needs by consuming the energy that has been stored by the plant. Photosynthesis is essential for life, as it is the only means by which extra energy (in the form of sunlight) can be introduced into the Earth. Without sunlight, life on Earth would be limited to communities of organisms such as those that rely on bacteria to harness **chemical energy** from volcanic vents on the ocean floor.

An incidental benefit

Oxygen, a by-product of photosynthesis, is of great importance to nearly all living organisms, as it is needed to release energy from their food. Virtually all the oxygen in the atmosphere has come from photosynthesis.

Every second, the world's plants produce billions of tonnes of sugar using sunlight.

From forests to fossil fuel

Around 365 million years ago, during a time in the Earth's history called the Carboniferous Period, the first forests appeared. These swampy forests were unlike anything we know today because they had no trees. Instead there were tree-sized club mosses and ferns, some with trunks over 30 metres tall, competing for light. Much of what would one day be North America and Europe was covered in fern forests. These forests would have been gloomy places, home to giant cockroaches, dragonflies as big as seagulls and scorpions, spiders and amphibians that scratched in the muddy forest pools. Flowering plants and birds had not yet evolved to bring colour and song.

Peat

There was not enough oxygen in the muddy forest pools to support the microscopic **decomposers** that usually break down plant and animal remains. As a result, when the plants of the swamp forests died, they did not completely decay, but were instead buried under layer upon layer of mud. Over the years, the partly decomposed dead plant matter was compressed into a substance called **peat**. Peat still forms today where the conditions are right, and is cut and dried for fuel in many places.

Coal is formed over millions of years as ancient plant remains are compressed deep underground.

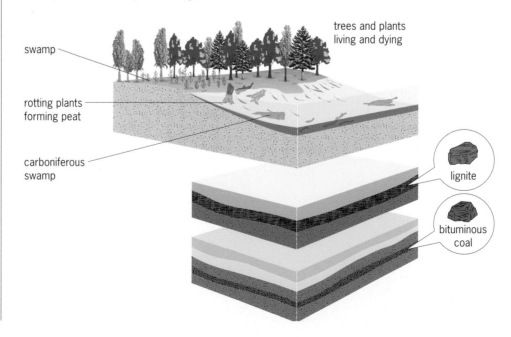

swamp

trees and plants living and dying

rotting plants forming peat

carboniferous swamp

lignite

bituminous coal

Sedimentary rocks

Over time, the peat deposits were buried under sand or other rocky materials. As these **mineral** deposits built up, the increasing pressure turned the deeper layers into rocks such as sandstone and shale. Rocks formed from mineral deposits in this way are called **sedimentary rocks**. The weight of the rock layers pressing down on the peat began the process that transformed it into coal as the temperature and pressure grew.

Coal formation

The buried peat deposits first produce a dark brown type of coal called lignite. Plant material is still recognizable in lignite. With further increases in pressure, the lignite turns into harder bituminous coal. Intense pressure at the deepest levels changes bituminous coal into anthracite, which is the hardest of coals. As you would expect, anthracites are the oldest coals, found deepest in the earth, and lignites are the youngest. Anthracites are over 300 million years old, whereas some lignites formed from plants growing within the last million years or so.

Coal composition

Coal is often referred to as a mineral but it has no fixed chemical formula, unlike a true mineral. Coal is chiefly composed of the elements carbon, hydrogen, nitrogen, oxygen and sulphur, but the actual amounts of each element can vary greatly. Coal is usually classified according to how much carbon it contains: anthracites are about 98 per cent carbon whereas lignites have a carbon content as low as 30 per cent. Anthracites and bituminous coal have a moisture content of about 1 per cent, lignites as much as 45 per cent. The way in which coal is used depends on its chemical composition and on how much moisture it contains.

Samples of anthracite, the oldest and hardest of the coals.

Compact coal

Over 2 metres of compacted plant matter will eventually produce a **seam** of bituminous coal less than a third of a metre thick.

Sea-life energy

Petroleum, or **crude oil**, was almost certainly formed from the remains of tiny organisms that lived in the world's oceans millions of years ago. Scientists came to this conclusion because they found carbon **compounds** in oil that could only have come from once-living organisms.

Oil formation

Millions of tiny organisms live in shallow water near the coasts or close to the surface in the deep ocean. As these organisms die, their remains sink through the water to settle as sediments (sand and silt) on the seafloor. Gradually, over a long period, this mixture of sediments and **organic** remains grows thicker.

As the deposits become deeper, the lower layers are subjected to increasingly high temperatures and pressure, and are squeezed together to form **sedimentary rock**. The extreme conditions cause chemical changes in the organic remains, resulting in the formation of a waxy substance called kerogen. At a temperature of around 100°C kerogen separates into liquid oil and **natural gas**. At greater depths, where the temperature rises above 200°C, the chemical bonds holding the **molecules** of the oil together begin to break down. So, if the temperature is lower than 100°C, little oil forms. If it is higher than 200°C the oil decomposes. The temperature range between these extremes, in which oil can form, is called the oil window.

Oil can only be reached by drilling through the **impervious** rock layers it is trapped beneath.

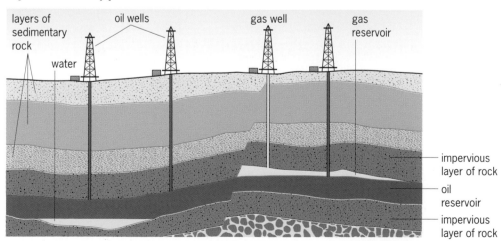

layers of sedimentary rock   oil wells   gas well   gas reservoir

water

impervious layer of rock

oil reservoir

impervious layer of rock

Pores and reservoirs

Sedimentary rock is filled with tiny cracks and holes, called pores. Oil and gas travel up through these pores, perhaps as a result of water in the rock pushing the oil upwards or because pressure from the rocks above squeezes the oil into the pores. As the oil and gas move upwards through the pores, they eventually reach a layer of impervious rock that they cannot pass through and so collect beneath it in a layer of **porous** rock called a reservoir.

Some reservoirs form near the Earth's surface but most are hidden deep underground. Although all oil reserves began beneath the seafloor, movements of the Earth's crust over millions of years have meant that many places that were once ocean floor are now dry land. For example, more than a hundred million years ago the deserts of the Middle East were beneath the Tethys Sea. These movements of the Earth's crust can sometimes bring oil reservoirs to the surface and the oil appears on the ground as **seepages** or springs. In Venezuela and Trinidad, lakes of oil have collected at the surface.

Oil rigs on Lake Maracaibo in Venezuela.

A continuing process

The process of oil formation continues today as sediment beneath the ocean floor is acted on by the same conditions of heat and pressure that formed oil millions of years ago. However, it will take millions more years to complete the process and we are using oil much faster than it is being formed.

King coal

Coal is a useful fuel. The amount of **heat energy** produced when a given amount of coal is burned is called its **heating value**. High-moisture coals, such as lignites have a lower heating value than anthracites and bituminous coals. Bituminous coals are by far the most plentiful and widely used types of coal. They have a slightly higher heating value than anthracites and are the only coals suitable for making **coke**. Anthracites burn too slowly for industrial purposes such as generating electricity, so bituminous coals are preferred. Coal is not a pure fuel and has many impurities, one of which is sulphur. As coal is burned, most of the sulphur combines with oxygen and forms poisonous sulphur dioxide gas. High-sulphur coals can cause serious pollution problems if burned without safeguards that remove the sulphur dioxide. Some of the ash left behind when coal is burned may also escape into the air, adding to air pollution. Filters are used to trap the ash in smokestacks and prevent it from reaching the air.

Native Americans in what is now British Columbia, Canada, burning coal for warmth.

Using coal

In many parts of Europe and Asia coal is still widely used for heating homes and other buildings. Anthracites are the cleanest-burning coals, and for this reason they are the best coals for heating homes. Unfortunately, anthracites are also the most expensive coals and so bituminous coals are often used instead to heat factories and other large commercial buildings. Coals with a low heating value, such as lignites, are rarely used for domestic heating.

Raw materials

The energy from coal is used in the manufacture of a wide variety of products, and many substances made from coal are used as raw materials. Coke, for example, is made by heating bituminous coal to about 1100°C in an airtight oven. Keeping oxygen out prevents the coal from burning and the heat causes some of the impurities in the coal to boil off as gases. Coke is mainly used in the manufacture of iron and steel.

When some of the gases produced during coking cool they turn into liquid ammonia and coal tar. Further processing can produce a light oil from some of the other gases. Ammonia, coal tar and light oil are used to make such products as drugs, dyes and fertilizers. Coal tar is also used for roofing and road surfacing.

Coal gas is also produced in coking. This burns like **natural gas** but it has a lower heating value and gives off large amounts of soot as it burns. It is sometimes recycled to provide heat for coking. It is possible to make high-energy gas and liquid fuels, such as gasoline and fuel oil, from coal, but this is a costly and complex process.

First fires

We will never know who first discovered that coal could be burned to provide heat. The world's first coal industry was established in China by the fourth century AD. The coking process was developed by brewers in the 17th century who used coke to dry malt for brewing. In 1709 Abraham Darby, an English ironmaker, devised a way to produce coke commercially and began to use it to **smelt** iron.

A coking plant in Pennsylvania, USA.

Discovering petroleum

The word **petroleum**, comes from two Latin words meaning 'rock oil' and people have been using oil from rocks for thousands of years. The ancient Egyptians coated mummies with pitch, a sticky black substance made from coal tar, which is obtained from bituminous coal. Pitch was also used in ancient times to make wooden ships watertight. Native Americans used **crude oil** for fuel and to make medicine centuries before European settlers arrived. In the eastern United States the remains of oil wells indicate that Native Americans knew how to get oil from underground deposits.

By the mid-18th century, the American colonists had found many oil **seepages** around New York, Pennsylvania and West Virginia. Some wells that were dug for salt produced oil, which was regarded as a nuisance. In the 1840s Abraham Gesner, a Canadian **geologist**, discovered kerosene. With the growing popularity of this fuel, which could be obtained from coal or oil, oil became more valuable.

Edwin Drake's oil well at Titusville, Pennsylvania.

Birth of the oil industry

In 1859 Edwin L Drake, a former railway conductor, drilled a well near Titusville, Pennsylvania. People called it 'Drake's Folly', not believing that he would find anything. However, Drake struck oil. Wooden **derricks** sprang up all over the hills of Pennsylvania as other prospectors began to drill wells nearby. Within three years, so much oil was being produced that the price of a barrel fell from $20 to 10 cents. To begin with, wagons and river barges carried the oil to refineries, but soon railway lines had to be laid to the oilfields to transport the growing quantities of oil. In 1865, the first successful oil pipeline was built to carry oil eight kilometres from Titusville to the nearest railway link. Within ten years, a 100-kilometre pipe took oil to Pittsburgh.

The industry grows

In 1860, Italy became the next country to produce oil, followed by Canada, Poland, Russia, Venezuela, Indonesia, Mexico and several other countries. The first oilfields of the Middle East were discovered in Iran in 1908, in Iraq in 1927 and in Saudi Arabia in 1938.

At first, kerosene was the chief product of the petroleum industry. Petrol, or gasoline, was just a useless by-product that was dumped, often straight into rivers. At the beginning of the 20th century this changed with the arrival of electric lights and the automobile. Suddenly gasoline wasn't useless any more. The introduction of the 'thermal-cracking process' in 1913 meant that the larger hydrocarbon **molecules** present in petroleum could be split into the smaller gasoline molecules. This boosted the amount of gasoline that could be obtained from crude oil from 11 barrels of gasoline out of every 100 barrels of crude oil to well over 20.

Supplies of petroleum were vital for the armed forces in the Second World War.

The First World War (1914–18) saw a huge increase in demand for petroleum fuels to power ships, trains, trucks and aircraft. After the war, many more farmers in the United States and Europe began to use tractors and other oil-powered equipment. The Second World War (1939–45) caused another huge increase in the production of petroleum as more oil products were needed for fuels and lubricants, and after the war the demand for petroleum products kept on growing.

Natural gas

Natural gas is easily distributed by means of pipelines and can be used for a wide variety of purposes, such as heating and cooking in homes and businesses. It has several advantages over other fuels. It can be quickly lit and just as quickly extinguished and can be burned in large or small volumes, allowing the consumer to make fine temperature adjustments. In comparison to coal and oil, natural gas produces much less pollution when burned.

Finding natural gas

Natural gas forms beneath the Earth's surface over millions of years as part of the same process that forms **petroleum**. This means that oil and natural gas are often found together, with the natural gas on top of the oil deposit or dissolved in it.

Natural gas is found in **porous** rocks such as limestone and sandstone. A dome of **nonporous** rock, such as a **salt dome**, forms a cap over the gas-bearing rock, trapping the gas. The gas cannot escape until a drill opens a hole through the solid rock.

Drilling for gas uses the same methods as those used in drilling for oil. The most common method being **rotary** drilling. Offshore gas wells are drilled in water as much as 2400 metres deep. Offshore drillers work from a barge, a movable rig or a fixed platform. Offshore drilling costs more than drilling on land, but it is usually much more productive. Some of the richest offshore gas-producing areas are the Gulf Coast waters off the United States and the North Sea around Europe.

A crew drilling for natural gas fit drill pipes together.

The gas industry

The natural gas industry began in the United States, taking off in the late 1920s with the development of improved pipes that could carry gas great distances economically. Up until the 1960s little natural gas was available in Europe. But, with the discovery of gas fields in the North Sea and in the former Soviet Union, the natural gas industry expanded rapidly. The world's largest known gas field was found in the Soviet Union in 1966.

Explosive power

In 1967 a hydrogen bomb with an explosive power equivalent to over 26,000 tonnes of TNT was detonated 1300 metres underground in the San Juan Basin of northwestern New Mexico. The explosion made gas deposits available that had been trapped in rock formations that were too hard for normal drilling.

A drilling rig in the rich gas fields of the Gulf of Mexico.

Gas distribution

Natural gas has to be cleaned and treated when it leaves the well. It is first taken to an extraction unit where impurities are removed. Next it may be taken to processing plants, where butane, propane and ethane can be taken out. The processed natural gas is then fed under high pressure into underground transmission pipelines to the consumers. The pressure of the gas drops as it is used up, and because of friction against the pipe walls. Compressor stations build the pressure up again.

Gas mains are large pipes connected to the transmission pipelines. Smaller pipes, called service lines, branch off from the mains, carrying the gas to consumers in homes, factories, schools, and other buildings. Because pure natural gas has no smell, a chemical is added to make it smell so that gas leaks are more noticeable.

Working in a coal mine

Thousands of miners – men, women and children – have been killed in mine accidents and many thousands have died of lung diseases as a result of breathing in coal dust. All large-scale early mining was done by hand, using picks and bars to remove the coal from the solid rock. In the 19th century, when demand for coal was soaring, many miners worked underground for over ten hours a day, six days a week. Once extracted, the coal was hauled to the surface by humans or animals such as dogs, ponies and horses.

Children as young as ten wheeled the coal from the mines in the 19th century.

Explosives were introduced to blast the coal in the late 18th century. In the late 18th and 19th centuries steam power for transport and pumping water from mines greatly improved underground coal mining. Today, most of the work in coal mines is carried out using machines. Although safety has been improved, coal mining is still hazardous.

Modern methods

There are three main methods of reaching an underground coal **seam**. Where a seam is exposed to the surface, on the side of a hill or mountain, a mine can be dug directly into the coal seam. This is the easiest and least expensive method. Alternatively, an inclined opening is dug through the surrounding rock to reach the coal seam, or a vertical mine shaft is dug down to the seam. Once the seam has been reached a variety of methods are used to get the coal out.

In conventional mining, the coal is first cut using a large chainsaw on wheels called an undercutter. Explosives are put into holes drilled into the coal, and detonated to dislodge the coal from the seam. The coal is loaded into a shuttle car that takes it to a conveyor belt for transportation to the surface. Roof support for the mine is provided by wooden timbers, steel beams set on posts or by steel rods anchored into holes drilled in the roof.

The continuous mining system uses a single machine that does the job of the undercutter, drills, explosives and loading machine. Other machines include the boring machine which cuts or breaks the coal using arms that rotate against the coal face. A ripper, which is similar to an undercutter, cuts the coal using chains on the coal face and can load the coal that it cuts. A milling or drum miner cuts the coal with drill bits mounted on rotating drums that are vertically parallel to the coal face. Drum miners are widely used.

In longwall mining, large exposed blocks of coal, 100 to 200 metres in width, are extracted. **Hydraulic jacks** provide roof support during mining. These jacks advance as the coal is mined and the roof behind the jacks is allowed to collapse. A conveyor belt transports the broken coal to the surface.

Strip mining

Strip mining, or surface mining, began in about 1910 when steam shovels were first being used. Today, 60 per cent of all coal is mined by this method. Often the coal deposit is covered by soil, which must first be stripped off, usually by large machines, such as bucket-wheel excavators. The coal is then broken up by explosives.

No matter how sophisticated the equipment, mining is still hazardous.

Searching for oil

Before about 1900, oil prospectors drilled where they found an oil **seepage**, and hoped for the best. Their equipment was little more than a pick, a shovel and perhaps a divining rod (a forked stick that some believed would magically lead them to the right place). In the 20th century, however, oil exploration became more of a science as **geologists** built up an understanding of how and why oil deposits are formed.

A nineteenth century engraving shows men being swamped by the gusher as Drake's Folly strikes oil.

Oil and geology

Oil geologists try to determine where oil might be found by studying rock formations. First an area is selected that might be promising, for example where there are **sedimentary rocks**. Then a detailed map is made of the area using photographs from satellites and aircraft, and observations carried out on the ground. The map is studied for signs of possible oil traps. A low bulge might be caused by a **salt dome**, a common **petroleum** trap, for example.

The next stage is to take cores, cylindrical samples cut through the layers of rock in an area. The geologists examine the structure and chemical make-up of the core. **Geophysicists** can locate geological structures that may contain oil with the aid of special instruments such as gravimeters, magnetometers and seismographs.

The gravimeter, or **gravity** meter, measures the pull of gravity at a particular location. Different kinds of rocks have different effects on gravity, for example, **nonporous** rocks tend to increase gravitational pull, while **porous** rocks tend to decrease it. Low readings on a gravimeter might indicate the presence of porous rocks, such as sandstone, which could contain oil.

A magnetometer measures changes in the Earth's **magnetic field**. The magnetic field, like gravity, is affected by the type of rocks beneath the surface. Sedimentary rocks usually have weaker magnetic fields than other types of rock. This difference allows potentially oil-bearing sedimentary rocks to be identified.

Seismographic surveys

A seismograph measures the speed of vibrations travelling through the Earth, either from an earthquake or from an underground explosion. Geophysicists can map the depth and shape of many potential oiltraps by recording the changing speed of the vibrations as they travel through rocks. To avoid using explosives to produce vibrations, geophysicists will sometimes use a thumper truck that strikes the ground repeatedly with a large metal plate.

Seismographic surveys can also be carried out at sea. A pulse of compressed air or an electronic pulse is sent out from a ship into the water. The waves from this pulse are reflected back from underwater features and recorded.

Seismographs allow geologists to look for fluids, such as oil or gas, in rock formations under the ground by using a technique called bright spot technology. Highly sensitive recorders are used to pick up changes in the height of the vibration waves as they are reflected from rocks that contain fluids. These variations appear as bright spots on the wave patterns recorded by the seismograph.

Thumper trucks (so called because they 'thump' the ground to create artificial seismic vibrations) being used in the search for oil in the desert of Libya.

Drilling for oil

No matter how thorough a geological survey of an area, there is still only one chance in ten that oil is actually found when the drilling begins, and only one chance in fifty that it will be there in amounts to justify the cost of extraction.

Preparing the site

Using bulldozers, a drilling site on land is first of all levelled and cleared. Roads are built to transport personnel and heavy equipment to the site. Supplies of water and power are provided, along with living accommodation for the workforce if there are no towns nearby. The oil rig, which consists mainly of drilling equipment and a **derrick**, will arrive by truck, barge or aircraft, depending on the accessibility of the site.

Rigging up

Connecting the parts of the oilrig is called rigging up. First, the construction crew erects the derrick over the spot where the well is to be drilled. Derricks range in height from 24 to 60 metres, depending on how deep the oil is believed to be. Hoisting machinery, for raising and lowering the drill in and out of the well hole, is attached to the derrick. Next, the engines that power the drill and other machinery are installed on the rig, as well as a variety of pipes, tanks, pumps and other equipment. After the drill is attached to the hoisting machinery, the well hole can be started, or 'spudded in'.

Drilling

Cable-tool drilling uses a steel cable to drop and raise on to the ground repeatedly a heavy cutting tool called a bit. Each time the bit drops, it cuts deeper into the earth. This method is best suited to digging shallow wells in hard rock. Bits may be over 2 metres in length and over 30 centimetres in diameter. Every so often, the cable and drill bit are removed and water is poured into the hole. The water and particles at the bottom of the hole are scooped out using a long steel pipe called a bailer.

Rotary drilling uses a bit attached to the end of a series of connected pipes, called the drill pipe. As the drill pipe is lowered into the ground, it is rotated and the bit cuts into the rock.

Different bits are used for hard and soft rocks. As the hole becomes deeper, extra lengths of pipe can be added. Drilling mud is pumped down the drill pipe and flows out of the openings in the bit and back up between the pipe and the wall of the hole. This mud cools and cleans the bit and carries soil and rock from the drill hole to the surface. The pressure of the mud in the well reduces the risk of blowouts and gushers, which are caused by the sudden release of pressure in an oil reservoir. Blowouts and gushers waste oil and may even destroy the rig.

Workers add piping to an oilwell in Wyoming, USA.

Changing the bit

The drilling crew changes the bit when it becomes blunt or if a different type is needed. To change the bit, they must pull out the entire drill pipe, which may be more than 7,620 metres long.

Offshore operations

Offshore oil explorations are much more difficult and dangerous than drilling operations on land. Crew and equipment must be transported to the site by helicopter or ship. In waters such as the North Sea and the Arctic Ocean, oil rigs may be damaged by storms or sea-ice. On average it costs ten times more to set up an offshore rig than to construct one on land. About one third of the world's oil comes from offshore oilfields.

Drilling offshore

Drilling an offshore well is similar to drilling a well on land. The parts of the drilling rig are the same, but the rig must be mounted on something that can be taken to sea. Wells drilled to explore a site are placed on movable rigs, such as jack-up rigs and semisubmersible rigs, or on drillships. A fixed platform is used when oil has been found and a well comes into production.

Jack-up rigs: These are commonly used in depths of up to 60 metres although they can be used in up to 110 metres of water. Jack-up rigs are so-called because they sit on a floating platform attached to steel legs that can be jacked up or down. When the rig is moved the legs are jacked up off the seafloor, the platform is lowered into the water and boats tow it to a new site. Once in position, the legs are lowered to the seafloor again and the platform is raised above the surface.

Semisubmersible rigs: These are used to explore for oil in depths of up to 1200 metres. The rig is mounted on a pontoon suspended just beneath the surface of the ocean. Anchors hold the rig in position.

Drillships use satellite navigation to stay in position over a deep-water wellsite.

Drillships: Drillships are used in water up to 2400 metres deep. The **derrick** and other drilling equipment are mounted on the deck of the drillship, and the drill pipe is lowered through an opening in the bottom of the ship. Onboard computers take readings from navigation satellites and make minute adjustments using the ship's engines to maintain a precise position over the drilling site.

Production platforms

Production platforms are only built and put in position after explorations have uncovered a reserve of oil large enough to justify the cost. Most fixed platforms are used in shallow water, but they can be used in depths of 300 metres or more.

Production platforms are built in segments that are taken to the drilling site in barges. The bottom segment is guided and lowered to the seafloor with cranes and secured to the seafloor with giant stakes, called piles. A second segment is fitted on top of the bottom segment. Some production platforms have three segments. The top segment is the base for the drilling operations. More than 40 wells can be drilled in various directions from a production platform.

An oil production platform in the North Sea burns off excess gas from the well.

Oil strike!

Drilling for oil is expensive and time-consuming. Throughout the drilling operations, the riggers (crew of a rig) look carefully for evidence of **petroleum** in the pieces of rock brought up by the drilling mud. When the depth likeliest to hold an oil deposit is reached, further tests are carried out.

Testing for oil

Coring involves replacing the drill bit (cutting tool) with a coring bit. A coring bit cuts out a cylinder of rock that can be brought up to the surface for analysis. Another test involves lowering measuring instruments, called sondes, into the well hole. They transmit information about the composition, fluid content, and other features of the underground rock. Riggers will also take samples of fluids and measure their pressure in the drill hole. If no evidence of oil is found, the well may be plugged with cement and abandoned.

Casing

If a productive well is found, the drilling crew removes the drill pipe and lowers steel casing (a steel pipe) into the well hole. Wet cement is pumped down the casing and covered with a special plug that can be drilled through. While the cement is still wet, mud is pumped into the casing and the plug is pushed to the bottom. The cement is forced up from the bottom of the hole to the surface, filling the space between the well hole and the outside of the casing. Once the cement has hardened the riggers can carry on drilling through the plug.

Riggers in China work to control a gushing oil well.

The steel casing acts as a protective lining for the well hole, helping to prevent leaks and the possible collapse of the hole. At the top of the casing, the drilling crew fits a blowout preventer, a giant valve that closes off the casing if pressure builds in the well.

Coming into production

Bringing the well into production is carried out in several steps. First, the crew lowers an instrument called a perforator into the casing. When it reaches the depth where the oil has been found, the perforator fires explosive charges into the casing, punching holes into it through which the oil can enter. Next, the crew installs tubing. This is a string of smaller pipes that conducts the oil to the surface. The casing itself would be too wide to get the oil flowing up fast enough. Tubing is also easier to repair and replace than the steel casing.

Finally, a group of control valves is assembled at the upper end of the casing and tubing to control the flow of oil to the surface. Because of its many branch-like fittings, this valve assembly is known as a 'Christmas tree'. More than one oil-bearing zone may be found where a well has been drilled. In this case the crew will install separate tubing and control valves for each zone.

Valves for controlling the flow of lubricants to a North Sea oil rig.

Power stations

Life for us without electricity is hardly imaginable. Electricity heats and lights our homes and provides power for our computers, televisions, refrigerators and a variety of other appliances. Machinery in factories, offices and hospitals also relies on electric power. Virtually all the electricity we use is produced by huge electricity generators in power stations, and most of these power stations are burning **fossil fuels** (coal, oil or **natural gas**) to operate the generators. Fossil-fuel power stations generate over 60 per cent of the world's electric power.

Superheated steam power

In the power stations the fuel is burned in a combustion chamber to produce heat, which is used to convert water in a boiler to steam. The steam flows through a set of tubes in a device called a superheater. The temperature and pressure of the steam in the tubes is raised by surrounding the superheater with hot gases from the combustion chamber.

An electricity generator inside a coal-burning power station.

The superheated, high-pressure steam is used to drive a huge steam **turbine**. A steam turbine consists of a series of wheels, each with many fanlike blades, mounted on a central shaft. As the steam flows through the turbine, it pushes against the blades, causing both the wheels and the turbine shaft to spin. The spinning shaft turns the rotor of an electricity generator.

An electricity generator has two main parts – a stationary part called a stator and a rotating part called a rotor. In the massive generators used in power stations, the stator consists of hundreds of windings of copper wire. The rotor is a large **electromagnet**. As the spinning shaft of the turbine turns the rotor, the **magnetic field** created by the rotor turns as the rotor turns. This spinning magnetic field produces a **voltage** in the wire windings of the stator, causing an electric current to flow.

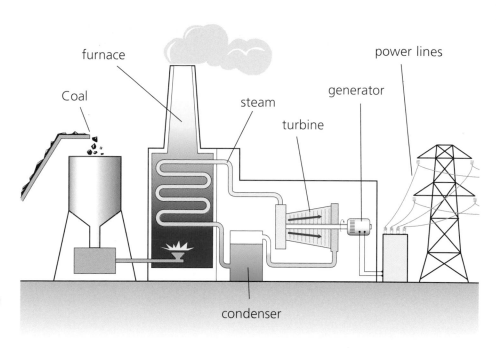

furnace

power lines

Coal

steam

generator

turbine

condenser

After the steam leaves the turbine it passes into a condenser where it flows around pipes carrying cool water. The heat from the steam is transferred to the water in the pipes and the steam cools, condenses into water again and is pumped back to the boiler in the furnace.

Spray ponds and cooling towers

The water in the condenser pipes, which has absorbed heat from the steam, has to be cooled before it can be used again. To do this, the heated water is pumped to a spray pond or a cooling tower. At a spray pond, the water is sprayed out through nozzles, which increases its surface area and therefore increases the rate at which it loses heat to the surrounding air. In a cooling tower the water spills down through a series of decks, cooling as it comes into contact with the air. The cooled water may be recycled through the condenser or simply discharged into a nearby lake or river, or into the sea.

Coal is burned to heat water to produce steam to spin a turbine to turn an electricity generator to produce electricity that we can use!

Pollution problems

Fossil-fuel power stations are a reliable way of producing huge amounts of electrical energy but they are not without their problems. Some power plants release heated water into the environment, which may harm plant and animal life, and the smoke from burning fossil fuels causes air pollution.

Moving the world

We depend on the internal combustion engine to make all the cars and trucks in the world move. A combustion engine burns a mixture of fuel and air, turning **chemical energy** into **heat energy**. The heat energy is then converted into **mechanical energy** to perform useful work.

Petrol engines

The most common kind of internal combustion engine is the petrol-powered piston engine, which uses petrol, or gasoline, obtained from **petroleum**. The rate at which a petrol engine produces work is usually measured in horsepower or watts.

There are two main types of petrol engine, reciprocating engines and **rotary** engines. Reciprocating engines have pistons that move up and down or back and forth. A crankshaft converts this reciprocating motion into rotary motion. A rotary engine, also known as a Wankel engine, after its inventor, Felix Wankel, uses rotors instead of pistons. The rotors produce rotary motion directly.

Petrol engines are well suited to powering vehicles because they are compact and light in weight for the power they produce. Nearly all cars, motorcycles and tractors have petrol engines, as do many trucks, buses, aeroplanes and some boats.

The four-step process by which an internal combustion engine works.

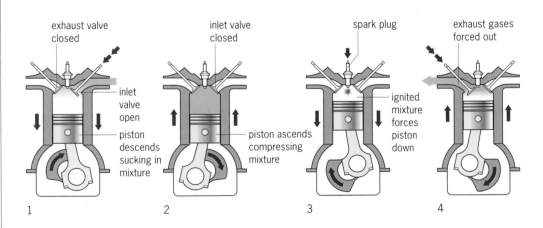

exhaust valve closed — inlet valve open — piston descends sucking in mixture 1

inlet valve closed — piston ascends compressing mixture 2

spark plug — ignited mixture forces piston down 3

exhaust gases forced out 4

Car engines

Most car engines consist of several cylinders arranged in one or two rows, each containing a piston and a spark plug. A mixture of air and petrol is forced into the cylinder and compressed. Then a spark from the spark plug explodes the petrol mix, propelling the piston along the cylinder. The pistons are connected to a rod, called a crankshaft. As a piston slides down the cylinder, it makes the crankshaft turn. The engine is set up so that the pistons are fired down the cylinders one after another. In this way the crankshaft is kept turning. The crankshaft is connected to the wheels of the car by means of a series of gears so that the wheels turn as the crankshaft turns. The amount of power the engine produces is controlled by a throttle that regulates how much air and fuel enter the cylinder.

Diesel engines

Diesel engines are mainly used for heavy-duty work, such as powering locomotives, large freight trucks and buses, although some cars also use diesel engines. Diesel power is also used in ships and submarines and in emergency electricity generators. Diesel engines are larger and heavier than petrol engines of equivalent power. They burn fuel oils, which, like petrol, are obtained from petroleum, but require less refining and are cheaper to produce. The diesel engine compresses the air in the cylinders, causing the air temperature to rise. Fuel is then injected into the hot, compressed air and ignites immediately. As with a petrol engine, the resulting explosion pushes against pistons, forcing them along cylinders to turn a crankshaft.

Near-death experience

The diesel engine was invented by Rudolf Diesel, a German engineer, who patented his design in 1892 and built his first engine in 1893. The engine exploded and almost killed him.

Diesel engines are often used to provide the power for large trucks.

Fossil-fuelled flight

Without **fossil fuels** the air traffic that encircles the world today would not be possible. Aircraft use two main types of engines: reciprocating engines and jet engines, both using fossil fuels.

Piston power

Reciprocating engines, also called piston engines, are the most widely used type of aero-engine. Although not as powerful as jet engines they are still used in most light aircraft because they are more efficient at low speeds. An aircraft's reciprocating engine is similar to the one found in a motor vehicle. Both types burn a fine spray of petrol and air inside cylinders, using the explosion to drive pistons inside the cylinders up and down and rotate a crankshaft. In an aircraft, the rotating crankshaft turns the propeller, whereas in a car it makes the wheels spin.

Engine power

The most powerful reciprocating engines ever used on aircraft were the 2722-kilowatt engines of the American B-36 bombers which flew in the late 1940s.

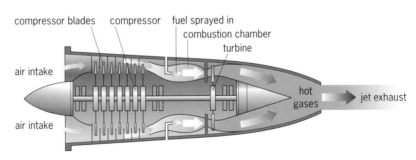

Cross-section through a jet engine.

Jet power

The principle of jet propulsion was first described in 1687 by Sir Isaac Newton in his third law of motion, which states that for every action there is an equal and opposite reaction. It is simply demonstrated by blowing up a balloon and releasing it. The air escaping from the balloon's neck is the action. The equal and opposite reaction is the wayward flight of the balloon around the room. Jet propulsion drives an aircraft engine in much the same way. Gas pressure inside the engine is produced by burning fuel in a combustion chamber. Most jet engines use a liquid **petroleum** fuel similar to kerosene. The gases are directed out through a nozzle as a powerful stream of jet exhaust that pushes the engine forwards.

34

Jet engines weigh less than reciprocating engines but produce much greater power, enabling large aircraft to travel long distances at high speeds. There are three main types of jet engines: turbojets; turbofans, or fanjets; and turboprops.

Turbojet: A turbojet takes air in through the front and burns it with fuel to give a powerful jet exhaust that thrusts the aircraft forward. As the jet exhaust passes out through the engine's tail pipe, it spins a turbine that turns a compressor, raising the pressure of the air in the engine. The turbojet was the first successful jet engine and is still used today.

Turbofans: A turbofan operates in a similar way to a turbojet, but it has a fan at the front that draws in air. Part of the air sucked in by the fan is burned with the fuel and the rest is added to the exhaust as it passes from the tail pipe. This results in an exhaust that is much cooler than that of a turbojet, but at the same time more powerful. Turbofans are more efficient at low speeds, quieter and use less fuel than turbojets. Almost all new commercial passenger jets have turbofan engines.

Turboprops: A turboprop, as the name suggests, is a combination of a turbojet and a propeller. The turboprop is basically a turbojet that uses its power to spin a power turbine that turns a propeller. The energy left in the combustion gases, after they have turned the power turbine, adds a small amount of jet thrust to the propeller's thrust. A turboprop combines the power of a jet engine and the stability of a propeller aircraft. Turboprops are smaller and lighter than piston engines but produce the same amount of power.

The fossil-fuel burning jet engine has revolutionized world transport.

Gas guzzlers!

A Boeing 747 can fly for 9700 kilometres on a single load of fuel (178,000 litres). This works out at just under 18 litres per kilometre!

The environmental impact

Removing **fossil fuels** from the earth and transporting them to wherever they are needed damages the environment. In strip mining (see page 21) earth-moving machines gouge holes in the ground, sometimes many kilometres across, to get at coal **seams**. Waste materials, called spoils, tend to produce acids when they are exposed to rain. Run-off from the strip mines may pollute nearby waterways as rainwater mixed with the acids runs down the bare slopes, also washing away fertile soils. Strip mining also results in fertile soil being buried under tonnes of rock. Waste material from deep shaft mines has to be dumped in huge tips on land or disposed of in the sea.

Strip-mined land can be reclaimed by levelling the steep slopes formed by the spoils and replacing as much topsoil as possible so that the area can be replanted.

The biggest mines in the world are opencast strip mines where minerals lie near the surface.

Sometimes mines can subside. Removing large seams of coal from under the ground causes the layers of rock above the coal seam to collapse, causing damage to buildings, roads and underground pipes and cables. Agriculture can also be affected as drainage systems are disrupted.

In their search for **petroleum**, oil companies must build roads and erect temporary structures in places where there might be oil. In the United States, for example, a great deal of controversy has been caused by oil exploration in the delicate **ecosystem** of the Arctic tundra. Leaks from wells drilled in shallow coastal waters create oil slicks that pollute beaches and kill sea-life.

Oil spills

In December 1999 the 25-year-old tanker *Erika* broke in two, spilling more than 10,000 tonnes of fuel oil on French beaches. This is just one of a number of incidents in which coastlines have been badly polluted by oil spills.

In the United States, the Oil Pollution Act (OPA) was enacted in 1990 after the *Exxon Valdez* oil spill caused huge environmental damage in Alaska. This legislation demands the use of double-hulled vessels, which are believed to reduce the chances of pollution in low-impact collisions or groundings. Operators have been given until 2015 to upgrade their fleets.

In Europe, single-hull crude tankers above a certain weight will not be able to enter European ports after 1 January 2010 if proposed regulations become law. Although all new tankers have been built with double hulls since 1996, the new regulations would still make up to 50 per cent of ships redundant.

Oil spills waiting to happen?

More than 2000 million tonnes of crude and refined oil products were transported globally by sea in 1998.

Volunteers begin the difficult task of cleaning up after an oil spill on the coast of France.

Pollution and climate change

The major sources of air pollution are cars, trucks, buses, factories and **fossil fuel** power stations. Air pollution contaminates the air with chemicals that can cause damage to **ecosystems**, are hazardous to health and generally make life less pleasant.

Acid rain

Acid rain is caused when chemicals released into the air from vehicle exhausts and from coal-burning power stations dissolve in water in the atmosphere to form sulphuric and nitric acids. This makes rain, snow and fog more acidic than usual. Air currents can carry the acid many kilometres away from the site of the pollution before it falls and damages crops, trees, lakes and buildings.

Many lakes in Scandinavia, the northeastern United States and Canada are so acidic that fish can no longer live there. Acid rain can turn buildings and statues black and damage them by corroding metal, stone and paint. Monuments and statues that have survived erosion by the weather for hundreds of years are suddenly being eaten away.

Trees damaged by acid rain in Poland.

The greenhouse effect

The Earth's atmosphere contains gases called **greenhouse gases**. A greenhouse works by letting the Sun's rays pass through its glass, while preventing **heat energy** from passing back out. These gases let the Sun's rays pass through to the surface of the planet, but they prevent the heat reflected back from the Earth's surface from being radiated into space and so the atmosphere gradually warms up. This is why they are called greenhouse gases.

Carbon dioxide, a greenhouse gas, is present naturally in the atmosphere. However, burning fossil fuels also produces carbon dioxide. Carbon dioxide trapped beneath the ground in coal and oil reserves is now being released into the atmosphere at a phenomenal rate. About 7 billion tonnes of carbon dioxide from burning fossil fuels and deforestation are released annually. Natural processes, such as the absorption of carbon dioxide by trees, removes about half of this, but the remaining 3.5 billion tonnes remains in the atmosphere for 50 to 200 years. Therefore, the amount of carbon dioxide in the atmosphere keeps increasing.

Many scientists believe that rising levels of carbon dioxide and other greenhouse gases are causing the Earth's climate to become warmer. This effect is called global warming. As a consequence, the climate could become so warm that the sea level will rise as some of the polar ice-caps melt, and the water in the oceans will expand as it is heated. Many coastal settlements will then be flooded. The worst effects of global warming could bring devastating floods and storms to many parts of the world as weather patterns are altered, but such changes are unpredictable.

Many countries are working to reduce air pollution, for example through the development of vehicles that are more fuel efficient and so burn less petrol. More power stations and factories are installing filters on their smokestacks to trap harmful chemicals before they can enter the atmosphere.

Heavy traffic in Mexico City. Cars are one of the worst causes of pollution.

Nonrenewable resources

Fossil fuels are nonrenewable resources – once our stocks have been used up they cannot be replaced in the foreseeable future. As we have seen, the formation of **fossil fuels** is a continuing process, but it takes many millions of years to get from plant and animal life to coal, **petroleum** and **natural gas**. We are using these resources much faster than natural processes are replacing them. The world relies very heavily on fossil fuels and a great deal of effort will have to be made to find alternatives. Ordinary people can play a part, too, by being energy conscious. If we use less electricity, less coal will have to be burned to produce it. If we walk or cycle instead of taking car journeys everywhere, less petrol will be consumed, pollution will be cut and resources will be conserved.

Crisis? What crisis?

During the oil crisis of the 1970s (see pages 42–43), there was panic as people began to believe that the oil supplies were running dry and prices would go spiralling up forever. Between 1973 and 1998, world oil consumption rose by around 25 per cent to 26 billion barrels annually. At the same time, proven oil reserves (those reserves of oil available at existing prices and using existing technology) jumped more than 50 per cent to 1 trillion barrels.

One reason for this is a huge improvement in the technology used to find oil reserves. Three-dimensional computer-generated seismic maps of underground formations mean that the prospects of a discovery are improved and riggers drill fewer 'dry holes' than before. The development of horizontal drilling techniques mean that more oil can be recovered from known fields. A traditional vertically-drilled hole taps an oil reservoir at

A technician uses a computer to analyse data that could help to pinpoint the location of an oilfield.

only one spot, from top to bottom, while a horizontal drill can run along the length of a reservoir, allowing the oil to be removed more efficiently. Improvements in deep-water drilling techniques have opened new fields for exploration as oil companies can now drill in waters five times deeper than a few years ago.

Coal

Coal supplies are not under quite so much pressure as oil supplies. Coal remains a vital commodity, providing a quarter of the world's commercial energy needs. However, we still have an ample supply of coal. At current rates of production and consumption, the world's coal reserves should last for more than 230 years. Oil reserves on the other hand are expected to begin to run out in 40 years. Also, unlike oil which is concentrated in the hands of a few major producers, coal reserves are evenly spread across Asia, Europe and America.

A train carries a fresh supply of coal to a power station.

China, for example, has colossal coal reserves. However, whereas most of these are in the northern provinces, demand for energy is growing fastest in the south. Because of the difficulty of transporting coal by land, China actually has to import about 50 million tonnes of coal a year. Australia is one of the world's largest exporters of high-quality coal and recently big companies from the United States, Britain and South Africa have been buying shares in Australian coal-mining businesses.

Fuel wars

Oil currently provides between 40 and 50 per cent of the world's energy needs. If every nation that used oil could produce enough to meet its own needs things would be fairly simple. However, this is not the case. Nations that consume large amounts of oil do not necessarily produce large amounts. Large-scale oil consumers such as France and Japan with no supplies of their own have always imported their oil.

During the 1970s, the United States passed from being self-sufficient in oil to having to import more than half of its oil supplies. The so-called 'oil shocks' of that time came about with the setting up of the Organization of Petroleum Exporting Countries (OPEC), a group of the major oil-producing nations, which didn't include Mexico, the United States and the USSR.

OPEC takes control

In the 1960s the OPEC countries had begun to take over the control of their own oil production from private oil companies. In the early 1970s, OPEC raised prices on **crude oil** to levels that affected the economies of all oil-importing countries, especially developing countries. Oil-dependent economies, such as Japan, sank into recession. Higher prices for **petroleum**-based fertilizers meant that the cost of food production rose as well. The developed world had less money to spend on importing goods from the developing countries, as more of their finances were going into meeting the increased cost of oil imports. At the same time, the developing nations had to pay more for imported goods, as the cost of manufacturing rose with the increase in energy prices.

Motorists tend to panic buy, putting pressure on fuel stocks, at the first sign of an energy crisis.

These effects on the world economy show how dependent we are on maintaining our supplies of energy. Because coal reserves are much larger and more widely distributed than petroleum reserves, it seems unlikely that any organization could control coal production in the same way as OPEC controls the oil supply. However, increased use of coal will cause severe pollution problems.

A volatile situation

In 1998 oil prices dropped by about 50 per cent. An economic crisis in Asia slowed demand, while a mild winter in the United States had the same effect. Misreading the signs, OPEC increased production and found that the oil supply was outstripping the demand. In the United States exploration and drilling projects were postponed or stopped altogether and 65,000 jobs were lost in the American oil industry alone. Other oil-producing nations also suffered huge losses.

In March 1999 OPEC cut output by 1.7 million barrels a day. Four non-OPEC nations (Mexico, Russia, Norway and Oman) also agreed to cut their combined output by 400,000 barrels a day. Demand for oil improved as Asia recovered.

The problem for planners in the industrialized nations is that two-thirds of the world's known oil reserves lie in the Middle East – a region known for its unpredictable politics. Who knows what future upheavals could disrupt the flow of fuel to the developed world?

The oilfields of Kuwait were devastated by retreating Iraqi troops at the end of the Gulf War in 1991.

Fuel alternatives

Japan is less dependent on oil supplies than it was in the 1970s. More than a third of Japan's electricity is now supplied by nuclear reactors, compared with just 6.5 per cent during the 1970s oil crisis. Cleaner industries such as computer software development are growing, while oil-demanding manufacturing industries, like steel, are less important.

Fossil fuel statistics

World oil production

Countries with the largest proven crude oil reserves, 1996
(in millions of barrels)

Saudi Arabia	261,444
Iraq	112,000
United Arab Emirates	97,800
Kuwait	96,500
Iran	92,600

Countries with the greatest oil production, 1996
(in millions of barrels per day)

Saudi Arabia	8.1
Former Soviet Union	6.9
United States	6.5
Iran	3.6
China	3.2

- At the end of 1996, OPEC had proven reserves of 801,998 million barrels of crude oil. This amounts to 76.6 per cent of the world total.

- There are 11 members of the OPEC group: Algeria, Indonesia, Iran, Iraq, Kuwait, Libya, Nigeria, Qatar, Saudi Arabia, United Arab Emirates, Venezuela.

- The total world consumption of crude oil in 1996 was 71.7 million barrels per day (there are 159 litres in a barrel).

Natural gas production (in billion cubic metres per year)	
Russia	640
United States	505
Canada	128
Netherlands	87

World energy production

Energy is measured in joules. A joule is a small unit and energy is usually measured in kilojoules (thousands of joules) or larger. In the following tables figures are given in terajoules (tJ), one terajoule is a million million joules. A bolt of lightning unleashes around 0.003 terajoules of energy.

Energy production, 1998	
United States	76.6 million tJ
Russia	41.9 million tJ
China	39.5 million tJ
Saudi Arabia	21.5 million tJ
Canada	18.2 million tJ
Great Britain	12.1 million tJ

- The United States produces more energy and uses more energy than any other country in the world.

Energy consumption, 1998	
United States	98.5 million tJ
China	39 million tJ
Russia	27.4 million tJ
Japan	22.6 million tJ
Germany	15.2 million tJ
Canada	12.9 million tJ
India	12.2 million tJ
Great Britain	10.6 million tJ

Glossary

acid rain   rain made acidic due to the presence of sulphur dioxide from coal burning, and nitrogen oxides from car exhausts and other sources. These gases dissolve in the water vapour in the air, forming sulphuric and nitric acids.

atoms   smallest units of matter that can take part in a chemical reaction, and the smallest parts of an element that can exist

cells   smallest units of life capable of independent existence. All living things, with the exception of viruses, consist of one or more cells.

chemical energy   energy held in the bonds that hold atoms together in molecules. Chemical energy is released during a chemical reaction.

coke   solid fuel made by heating coal in an airtight oven to remove impurities. Coke is around 90 per cent carbon and the most commonly used fuel in the iron and steel industries.

compound   chemical substance made up of two or more atoms of different elements which are bonded together

crude oil   another name for petroleum

decomposers   organisms that break down dead matter

derrick   the tower used for hoisting drill pipes

ecosystem   community of living organisms together with their non-living environment

electromagnet   magnet produced by passing an electric current through a wire wrapped around an iron core

fossil fuels   fuels produced through the action of heat and pressure on the fossil remains of plants and animals that lived millions of years ago; the fossil fuels are coal, petroleum and natural gas

geologist   scientist who studies the origin, history and structure of the Earth

geophysicist   scientist who studies the branch of physics concerned with the Earth and its environment, including seismology (the study of earthquakes) and oceanography

geothermal   energy extracted from hot rocks below the Earth's surface

gravity   force of attraction between any two objects

greenhouse gas   gas in the atmosphere, such as carbon dioxide or water vapour, that absorbs heat radiated from the Earth's surface that would otherwise escape into space

heat energy   energy created by moving atoms and molecules

heating value   measure of the amount of energy produced when a fuel is burned

hydraulic jacks   device powered by water pressure and used for lifting heavy weights

impervious   something that cannot be penetrated

Industrial Revolution   period of history from around 1740 to 1850 when economic and social life in Britain, and later the rest of the world, was transformed by the introduction of coal-powered steam engines to drive machines for manufacturing

magnetic field   region around a magnet in which a force acts on another magnet or on a moving electric charge

mechanical energy   measurement of the amount of work that an object can do (a combination of the object's potential and kinetic energy)

micro-organisms   living organisms that are too small to be seen with the naked eye

mineral   naturally occurring solid inorganic substance with a definite chemical composition and a characteristic structure; also used to name any substance, such as coal, that is extracted from the ground

molecules   two or more atoms joined together by chemical bonds; if the atoms are the same it is an element, if they are different it is a compound

natural gas   mainly methane, the lightest of the hydrocarbons. Other gaseous hydrocarbons found in natural gas include ethane, propane and butane. Gases such as carbon dioxide, helium and nitrogen may also be present.

nonporous   describes a solid with few tiny holes or pores

organic   describes something that is derived from living or once-living organisms

peat   compacted plant remains that have partly decomposed in conditions of low oxygen

petroleum   thick, yellowish-black liquid mixture of hydrocarbons found beneath the surface of the Earth. It is formed by the action of bacteria, and the forces of high pressure and temperature, on the remains of marine plants and animals over millions of years.

photosynthesis   process by which green plants and some other organisms harness the energy of sunlight to make sugars from carbon dioxide and water

porous   describes a solid that has many tiny holes or pores through which fluids can pass

rotary   relating to rotation or spinning

salt dome   underground structure formed when salt layers penetrate denser material in the Earth's crust. Petroleum is often found near to salt domes.

seam   underground layer of a mineral such as coal

sedimentary rock   rock formed over millions of years by the accumulation of layer upon layer of sediments deposited by wind, water or ice

seepage   places where petroleum seeps out of the ground

smelt   obtain a metal by heating its ore (the rock from which the metal is obtained) to a high temperature

turbine   engine in which a fluid is used to spin a shaft by pushing on angled blades. Turbines are used to spin electricity generators.

voltage   measurement of the force that moves an electric current around a circuit

Index